by
George Fisher

Rose Publishing Co.
301 Louisiana
Little Rock, Ark. 72201

To Danny
J can recall many
discussions with you
relative to these
characters.
Sonny
12-25-80

Acknowledgments

I wish to thank the following people who contributed to the production of this book.

Jerry Dhonau

Jill Dixon

Ernest Dumas

Keith Essex

Dorothy Harwell

Nancy Johnston

James O. Powell

Connie Prescott

Mayme Rockenbach

Copyright 1978 by Rose Publishing Co., Inc.
ISBN 0-914546-21-X

Printed in the U.S.A.

FOREWORD
by James O. Powell

George Fisher is the complete Arkansan. Indeed, he is so much the native son and so much the creature of our celebrated hill country that one could suspect him...*dare* I say it?...of being a *professional* Arkansan, that is, one born in Peoria or even Lubbock. Usually it is the converted Arkansan who is fiercest in his identification with the Wonder State. But no, Fisher is for real, having been born in Searcy and reared in Beebe, and he cannot help singing folk songs and playing the pickin' bow when he is demonstrating the caricaturist's art, even if it does make his honoraria the envy of the rest of us. He is simply informal to a fault, as is suggested in the choice of his favorite restaurant, which is Grandpa's, a North Little Rock catfish house where the appetizers are unshelled peanuts and the patrons throw the hulls on the floor. Fisher keeps a cabin in Timbo, in the hills, and he would live there if it weren't for the blasted tranquility, which leaves him in a state of intolerable contentment. Deprive an editorial cartoonist of his daily sense of outrage and, in the case of Fisher, anyway, you deprive him of his inspiration, so Fisher has to live in Little Rock where as everyone knows you can muster at least two outrages a day, easy. That is one more than is needed to give the *Arkansas Gazette* its editorial page cartoon.

I have worked with Fisher regularly, if hardly systematically, for some seven years, and it hasn't been easy for either of us. At first he was doing two cartoons a week for us on the Opp Ed Page while he was running the Fisher Art Service, and then he became chief editorial cartoonist of the *Gazette* after determining that what he really loved to do most was what had been his sideline. What makes editors grow gray is Fisher's penchant for turning out now and then, slyly, a cartoon that, if published, would set off epidemic apoplexy amongst the paper's legal counsellors, or, on occasion, a cartoon that outrages our most sacred popular conventions even beyond the limits to which the *Gazette's* hardy subscribers are accustomed. These cartoons usually find their way to the famous Fisher *Salon de Refuse*, which is a popular feature of the Fisher exhibitions at the Arkansas Arts Center. My own favorite for the *Salon* is one that shows Barbara Jordan and Jimmy Carter, in full color, as madonna and child. The runner-up is Fisher's refinement of Rembrandt's *Anatomy Lesson;* in this one the cadaver is Governor David Pryor and the surgeons are State Senator Ben Allen and other state legislators who dispatched Pryor's proposed "Arkansas Plan" with such merciless precision in the 1977 legislative session.

Curiously, the funniest cartoons that Fisher and others draw derive from the classical allusion, like the two in the *Salon* that I have mentioned. For further illustration, in this book we have one of Fisher's most delightful, depicting Michelangelo's *Creation of Man*... only it is Coach Frank Broyles who is reaching down from the cloud to breathe life into Lou Holtz. Another of my favorites is the one showing Moses making his passage through the Red Sea... which the U.S. Engineers have just dammed on either side so he can get across. Still another has Prime Minister Menachem Begin as Moses coming off Mount Sinai with some new tablets on what is forbidden in Begin's Israel. But with the point made, let us not here reveal too much of the good clean fun and pungent commentary that lies in the ensuing pages.

This is Fisher's fifth book of his published cartoons. All have been popular. He got started with his books while he was drawing a cartoon every week for the *North Little Rock Times* which was picked up by newspapers all over the state, including the *Gazette*, which used it as a regular feature on the Sunday Opp Ed Page alongside the *Arkansas Press*. The collection of Fisher's work published here covers a full range of issues in politics and government, manners and morals. His commentary is local, state, national and international, for all good editorial car-

toonists have a world beat. The cartoons herein are assembled in categories, one group centered on environmental issues, another centered on the election year 1978, another on David Pryor's hair-raising adventures in the legislature with his celebrated Coon Dog Plan *(requiescat in pace)*, another a miscellany, and so forth. It isn't a bad idea to take the book a category at a time, one group at a sitting. The principle is rather like going to an art gallery and looking at a pre-arranged limited selection each day, but no more, lest the palate become sated as in drinking too much wine.

It is widely known, of course, that editorial cartoonists live in the best of all possible worlds. George Fisher can strip the hide off a misbehaving politician and the subject will often be on the phone the first day asking for a print to hang on the office wall. An editor can say the same sort of thing with words and the subject may appear forthwith with a horsewhip. Life isn't fair, really, like Jack Kennedy said. Anyway, the truth is that to be featured in a Fisher cartoon is something of a status symbol in Arkansas politics: it means that a man (woman) has arrived.

Fisher does have problems occasionally, like the prophet in his own country. He used to be invited to speak in Beebe now and then, but not so much since he drew a cartoon suggesting that his alma mater,

Beebe Branch of Arkansas State University, was something less than the new Athens. Fisher has always been hard on colleges of the community college genre; he says that he is an authority on the subject, having graduated from one.

What troubles Fisher most in his idyllic world is the loss of his best subjects as the Moving Finger writes. He complains nostalgically that the new breed of Arkansas politician is too scrubbed up, too nice looking. Possibly Fisher is like a veteran top sergeant remarking how it ain't like the Old Army, but, still, he has a point: Certainly there'll never be another Orval Faubus, nor is there any chance that Faubus will emerge from the obscurity that has swallowed him up following a succession of defeats. Nor will there be another Mutt Jones or Paul Van Dalsem, two celebrated legislators who have met their own Waterloo. In this book Fisher bids them a sentimental farewell in a cartoon waving them off to the Old Guard Rest Home, along with Orval and Bruce Bennett and other selected favorites who have gone to their political reward (with Fisher lending momentum to their early retirement).

It may seem that life for George Fisher is all fun and games, and certainly he has more than his share of good times. But Fisher's cartoons are sometimes dramatically somber, even melancholy, and even in employing his prevailing humorous style he has a deadly serious point to make, as a rule. Fisher is one of those cartoonists who never forget they are *editorial* cartoonists, not comic strip artists; he is one of those who have something important to say deriving from a set of convictions. Nor does Fisher select his targets just because they happen to be vulnerable; if Fisher lashes a public figure or public body it is because in his mind the target *deserves* the lashing. There are, alas, too many cartoonists, often running in a pack, who dash back and forth from one side of an issue to another because their purpose is simply to entertain, sometimes maliciously. Not Fisher. He can be hard on his adversaries, certainly, but he is *not* merely trying to divert his public; rather, he wants to lead his public toward the truth as he sees it, even if he leaves them laughing most of the way.

As a footnote, I would remark what many of Fisher's fans regard as obvious: he is not only a first-rank editorial cartoonist; he is one of the best in the country. Although widely reprinted, Fisher's work is not so well known as that of the "household names," like Conrad and Herblock, but it was only about two years ago that he turned full-time. He has the style and flair, I think, to make any sound list of the Top Ten.

●

James O. Powell is Editorial Director for the *Arkansas Gazette.*

A NEW COON DOG IN EVERY YARD

Pryor and his Coon Dog

David Pryor as governor has been a fiscal care-taker. He would like to be known as an innovator but many of his most publicized ideas either wouldn't fly or were shot down.

Most memorable among these was his so-called "Arkansas Plan," more widely known, after the smoke cleared, as the "Coon-dog" plan.

Its aim was to shift some of the state services and revenues to the county and city levels. His way of accomplishing it would be to cut state income taxes 25% and allow local governments to levy a sales tax or any other tax, which they could use to set into motion any program or services they wanted.

Pryor took to the road to sell his plan. In Jonesboro he made his fatal mistake. He wanted to describe it in such down-to-earth terms that any local tobacco-chewing whittler would understand it. He explained that his plan would reduce the pie in Little Rock and give it to local folks, letting local governments spend it on services of their choice, adding that that could be, if they so desired, a new shotgun or a coon dog.

June 15, 1975

"I think we need to open an office in Europe."

November 16, 1975

"Okay, we'll run it up the flagpole and . . ."

October 14, 1976

October 19, 1976

"Keep it—as a gift from us."

November 19, 1976

*"Now the time has come
to sign another important document—
will the sergeant-at-arms cover the exits?"*

November 24, 1976—Pryor began to notice that acceptance of his plan was a long, long way off.

*"Your competitor across the street says
it ain't new—he says it was once wrecked
by Ronald Reagan."*

December 1, 1976—Wall Street Journal wrote a story about Pryor's plan pointing out that it was very similar to the one Ronald Reagan had been trying to peddle.

Convert

December 14, 1976

9

December 24, 1976—Pryor's project was running into real trouble. He altered the plan to soften the resistance from schools, cities and counties. He proposed delaying the major impact of the plan until 1979 (when he would be out of office, critics said), by postponing the state tax cut until that year and restoring and even raising state aid to cities and counties for the intervening two years. To the relief of the Arkansas Education Association, he took the public schools out of the plan altogether. Most people regarded it as the same old dog.

Switching dogs in the middle of the street

December 19, 1976—Pryor has always advocated a new constitution. Constitutional reform may have solved many of the state's basic problems, but it seemed that the Governor was opting for his own idea.

Inaugural Address

January 12, 1977

"When a legislator gets out of line, just flash your teeth at him."

January 20, 1977

February 1, 1977

11

"Coonus Caninus Arkansus"

February 17, 1977

April 1, 1977

April 12, 1977

July 26, 1977—The General Assembly did give Pryor something. It passed his anti-litter program, which put a tax on certain businesses that produced litter. Howls went up all over the state when tax statements went out. Legislators immediately wanted to repeal it.

August 7, 1977—The law-makers got their wish when Pryor had to call the legislature back into special session to correct some General Assembly errors. They wasted no time in repealing the litter tax.

GALLERY

TOM BONNER

JOHN FOGELMAN

JUDY PETTY

RICHARD MAYS

FRANK BROYLES

GALLERY

HUGH B. PATTERSON

IRENE SAMUEL

BOB RILEY

JUDGE ERNIE WRIGHT

SAM HARRIS

15

"My compliments to the chef."

March 23, 1975

Two-ring Circus

The Arkansas Legislature spends about 72 days every two years in general assembly. The late Spider Rowland said he had a better idea. He suggested they meet 2 days every 72 years. They fight, fuss, fume and cuss, but after the cigar smoke clears away and waste baskets are emptied, they go back home having fulfilled (usually) their mission in some sort of fashion.

For as many years as I can recall, this body of law-makers never has received a high rating from the public. What is amazing to me is that they seem to be oblivious to this fact.

NEWS ITEM: Pryor foresees need for full-time legislature.

November 2, 1975

"Look boys! We'll just extend the old bench a little. What are rules for?"

February 2, 1975—Senators Walmsley and Douglas had a set-to about who should be on the prestigious Joint Budget Committee. The Senate easily settled the question by amending the rules so that both could serve on it. All were friends again.

February 16, 1975

Biennial Sop Pageant
January 27, 1976

"Last Time, It Was A Rope!"

February 1, 1976—Daisy Bates, president of the NAACP back in 1957, figured prominently in the struggle for desegregation. Speeches were made on the Senate floor denouncing her as a communist. Almost 20 years later, black Senator Jerry Jewell got a resolution through honoring her for her good works.

"That looks like it might be... yes, it is...it's Ole Paul!"

June 1, 1976—After Orval Faubus faded from the Capitol scene, the Old Guard Rest Home started filling up. Paul Van Dalsem, long a bruising legislator from Perry County, was beaten in the primary.

Many readers called for identification of the old timers on the porch. Most guessed the first two, (Faubus and Mutt Jones). The next two are Marion Crank and Bruce Bennett.

"My, grandmother—
what a big referendum you have."

January 18, 1977—The legislature wanted to refer the not-so-heated ERA question to the voters in a state election, but the bill finally died in committee.

"Smile! We're on National TV!"

January 25, 1977—Rep. Arlo Tyer from Pocahontas tried to get a bill passed requiring unmarried couples living together to pay a special tax. He also wanted to clean up dirty movies. The legislature voted down his ideas but not before they made the national TV news.

Trojan Truck

January 26, 1977—Every session, it seems, the truck lobby tries to push through a bill to allow longer and heavier trucks on our highways. The lobby failed in this session, too.

February 25, 1977—Rep. Boyce Alford of Pine Bluff didn't see the necessity of allowing too much public access to government records. His incredible remark shown in this cartoon was made on the floor of the House. This could have had something to do with his defeat in this year's primary.

The Joint Budget Committee is now in session.

March 10, 1977—The Joint Budget Committee came under fire from many fellow law-makers who claimed that the JBC alone decided how practically all state tax money was spent, leaving them virtually powerless. So the outs created a power base of their own, naming it The Legislative Joint Performance Review Committee.

March 3, 1977

June 2, 1977

July 24, 1977—Pryor had to call a mid-year special session to provide appropriations for kindergartens, which the General Assembly forgot to do a few months earlier. The question was, would the ever-present special interests muscle in and take advantage of this brief session?

August 4, 1977—The legislature wanted to use the special session for settling the constitutional reform question. It wanted a bill that would let the voters decide, but that was the job for law-makers. Just before the session convened, however, Pryor announced that he would go along with the legislature's plan.

August 9, 1977—The constitutional referendum bill to let the voters decide in the general election became a law.

News Item:
The Arkansas Legislative Council is concerned about the high cost of a new execution facility.
(Here are some suggestions)

December 7, 1977

"If you believe in peanut butter, you gotta believe in ME."

May 25, 1976

Born Again

The phenomenal rise of Jimmy Carter from a Peanut Farm to the White House will be studied by political scholars for a long time to come. Following Watergate, most people thought it was a lead-pipe cinch that a Democrat would be elected.

That's what happened all right—but by the skin of his teeth.

The Carter-Ford battle was a roller-coaster of ups and downs, bloops, blunders, promises, appeasement, tough talk, pious talk.

Ford had the incumbency going for him but that advantage was probably offset by the Nixon pardon. Many people preferred his wife, Betty.

Carter was an unknown quantity—many people worried about where he stood on various issues—but he just kept smiling and saying, "Trust me, I'll never lie to you."

July 15, 1976

September 11, 1974—On the same day Evel Knievel made his aborted jump across Grand Canyon, Ford granted Nixon a pardon. His popular rating plummeted.

"You won't catch ME doing something stupid like sawing myself off a limb."

March 19, 1975

Southern Strategy

September 7, 1975—Vice President Rockefeller wanted very much to be Ford's running mate, so he started a speaking and handshaking tour of the South, including Arkansas.

" 'BOO' WHO?"

October 28, 1975—Ford, as president, thought for a while he had the GOP nomination sewed up, but he couldn't scare Ronald Reagan enough to make him stay out of it.

January 7, 1976—Ford admired the late Harry Truman and didn't try to hide it.

The R. Reagan "Turn America Around" Plan

February 3, 1976—It was argued that Reagan's economic recovery plan would be helpful to some states but harmful to others. He replied to critics that if people in the adversely affected states didn't like it, they could "vote with their feet," and move elsewhere.

Detente

March 4, 1976—"Detente" was a special pet of Kissinger, who tried to keep it alive and well, but Reagan made it a dirty word (coddling the Commies, etc). Ford couldn't let Reagan get too far to the right of him, so he started kicking it around, too.

Strange Horse Race

March 9, 1976

Achilles Heel

March 24, 1976

Hard-Line Reverberation

April 2, 1976—Reagan stepped up his hard-line talk and Ford started sounding strangely like him.

Stars fell on Alabama

April 8, 1976—Democratic presidential candidate George Wallace kept losing primary after primary. He soon faded from the scene.

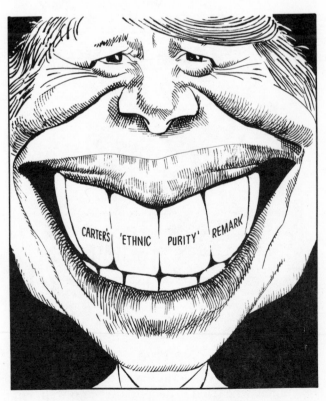

"Well shut mah mouth."

April 13, 1976

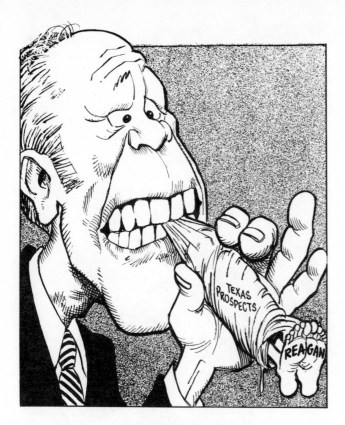

Tough tamale

April 28, 1976—On the campaign trail in Texas, Ford was offered a tamale. He tried to eat it shuck and all.

May 5, 1976— One of Wallace's problems was Reagan, who was winning over the old hard-liners that were once Wallace disciples.

"He wandered into a bar in North Carolina — then one thing led to another."

May 11, 1976—Reagan finally won a very important primary—from then on the party appeared addicted.

"Heal!"

May 20, 1976—Carter, too, ran into trouble. Senator Church beat him in a primary. Governor Jerry Brown also stepped in and clobbered Jimmy in several primaries, but key states like Pennsylvania, New York and Ohio were all that he needed to put him over.

Gift Horse

May 2, 1976

Little old lady in tennis shoes.

June 13, 1976

Puttin' it awl togethah

June 18, 1976

June 20, 1976

June 24, 1976

Born Again

July 18, 1976

"He'll get the hang of it. You don't learn to be a switch-hitter overnight."

August 5, 1976

It's beginning to look a lot like Ford

August 8, 1976

August 18, 1976

August 20, 1976

August 22, 1976

"If I hear 'detente' just once . . ."

August 25, 1976

"Look at it this way, John: You're getting the seeds."

August 26, 1976

September 3, 1976

"Why can't you emulate someone from your OWN party, suh?"

September 14, 1976

September 15, 1976

"Now let's see — do you suppose he can make a scene with his feet?"

September 28, 1976

October 1, 1976

September 24, 1976

"I bought it in '74 from Nixon — why do you ask?"

October 10, 1976

"Well, of all the nerve!"

October 13, 1976

*"Remember — your name is Gerald Ford
—you're happy to be in Duluth . . .
DU-LUTH. Just follow the script."*

October 20, 1976

November 5, 1976—Since 1968 the Arkansas Democratic Party has broken the row to graze in the neighbors' pastures, but Carter's Oats put it back where it traditionally has been. Arkansas gave Jimmy Carter the largest vote percentage of any state except Carter's home state of Georgia.

Time to re-tire.

October 31, 1976

"First, we knock some sense into its head, then we'll teach it obedience."

November 18, 1976—GOP right-wingers immediately started talking about revising the basic structure of their party. Some even wanted to change the name or even form a new party.

December 5, 1976

"I just don't understand why we don't get our share of the colored vote."

December 16, 1976—More than 90% of the Nation's blacks voted for Carter—a phenomenal percentage.

Bench Strength

December 17, 1976

June 18, 1978

June 29, 1978

GALLERY

EDDIE POWELL

JIMMY JONES

BRUCE ANDERSON

EDDIE SUTTON

J. GAYLE WINDSOR, JR.

GALLERY

ROBERT JOHNSTON

HENRY WOODS

JOHN WARD

G. THOMAS EISELE

TELLER

ERNEST GREEN
ASST. SECY.
OF LABOR

April 22, 1977—Many say that history should be written after 20 years. In 1957 Governor Faubus called out the Guard and blocked nine black teen-age students who attempted to enroll in Central High, according to the Little Rock School Board's court-approved plan. The first student to be turned back was Ernest Green. Twenty years later, Green visited Little Rock with the title of U.S. Assistant Secretary of Labor, while Faubus was a teller in a branch bank at Huntsville.

Twenty Years Since 'Central High'

Possibly no other major power since history began has attempted to turn itself around 360 degrees on the matter of race, based on conscience and law. In 1954, the United States Supreme Court said that the nation's schools could no longer be divided by race. Later, the courts included public as well as private facilities. This, I believe, our country had to do if it survived as a free and powerful nation.

The struggle to end racial barriers is not over, however, for in recent years we have witnessed the spectacle of the Burger Court turning itself around on matters of civil rights, as if it had not the slightest notion as to what this nation is all about.

Here are several cartoons dealing with courts, laws, race, and human treatment.

February 4, 1977

45

*"Don't think of me as a doting cynic—
Remember that I was kind to someone."*

January 4, 1976

*Some nations have been known
to liquidate their aged—
we just abandon them.*

July 3, 1977

*The Supreme Court Shuffle
(A new game where nobody wins)*

August 26, 1977

September 21, 1977

November 1, 1977—The Ku Klux Klan announced that its members would serve as volunteers to patrol the Mexican-U.S. border to help deter illegal aliens.

Oil in the Family

February 17, 1978—It was reported mysteriously that the policy-making board of NAACP was being packed with oil company personnel. NAACP explained that it had shifted policy. It said its people were the ones who were out of work and that government couldn't create jobs like big business could. "If you can't lick 'em...."

The Cross and the Flag

December 27, 1977

"It's old Earl — let him edge in, but save a
space for Henry."

October 8, 1976

Meanwhile,
Back in San Clemency

Not much needs to be written here about the chapter on Nixon and the post-Watergate period because you know the story backwards and forwards. Most of the Nixon men were convicted of crimes of one sort or another and many went to jail.

Nixon could be seen on rare occasions, such as his interviews with David Frost, but it was the same old Nixon. "If the president did it, that makes it legal."

"Now you have the trip to Russia; the diamond earrings, the $60,000 pension — would you like to continue or . . ."

August 7, 1974

49

"Friends! Who needs 'em — right, Bebe?
. . . Bebe?"

August 13, 1974

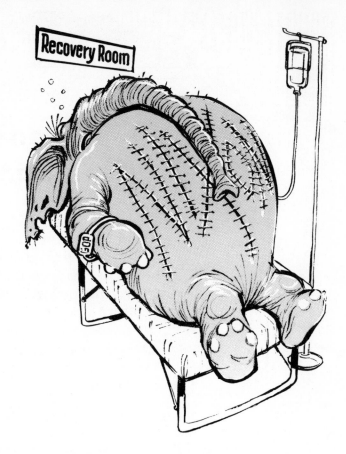

August 25, 1974

". . . and now, please — the rainbow?"

January 7, 1975

"Actually, very few persons have ever
come back a third time."

October 22, 1975

"There, but for the Grace of Gerald Ford . . . ."

February 25, 1975

"Now what this country needs is . . . are you listening to me?"

November 20, 1975

December 12, 1975

"Oh, I don't know — what do YOU want to talk about?"

February 25, 1976

The People's Republican of China

March 2, 1976

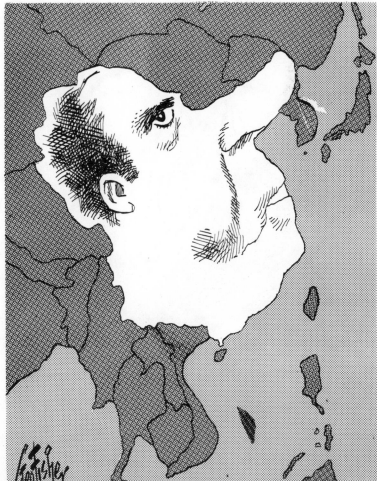

Meanwhile, back in San Clemency.

August 29, 1976

June 9, 1977

June 25, 1978

May 3, 1977—Nixon broke his long silence by appearing on television with David Frost in a much ballyhooed series of interviews.

GET ME RICHARD MILHOUS NIXON!

September 8, 1977—Throughout the TV series, Nixon kept absolving himself from Watergate guilt. But in the final interview he had it all nailed down—Martha Mitchell did it. He said that Martha had become emotionally unstable and John Mitchell found her too difficult to live with. This grieved John so much that it made him do all sorts of strange things—like hanging around with hoodlums and burglar types.

GALLERY

WITT STEPHENS

JOHN PAUL HAMMERSCHMIDT

DR. BESSIE MOORE

KURT KLIPPSTATTER

RICHARD ALLEN

HERBIE BYRD

"Do you suppose this means my sphere of influence has been limited, Mutt?"

January 26, 1974

The Rustication of Mutt & Marlin

Sheriff Marlin Hawkins of Conway County and former Senator Guy H. "Mutt" Jones of adjoining Faulkner County are colorful politicians who have dominated the political scene in their respective areas for many years.

Marlin announced that he would retire as sheriff and undisputed boss of the Conway County political organization after his current term ended. Mutt was retired by his own Senate colleagues in 1974 following a federal income tax fraud conviction. But he still keeps busy trying to get himself reinstated as a solid citizen.

As if these two old warriors couldn't provide enough entertainment for the twin counties, there's the court room of Circuit Judge Russell Roberts. Roberts is widely known for his controversial rulings and sometimes bizarre courtroom behavior. His methods of impaneling grand juries will be a source of conversation in the Fifth Judicial District for years to come. The judge has announced that he, too, will retire in January.

The Mad Hatter's Tea Party

April 27, 1975

59

"Election irregularities in MY county? Why doesn't someone tell me about these things?"

August 6, 1975

"Well, is our little ol' Grand Jury ready?"

December 28, 1975

March 24, 1977

News Item: Sheriff Marlin Hawkins wants to be director of Police Academy.

August 12, 1977

*"Just 'cause I ain't as big as I used to be,
Alex Streett keeps pickin' on me."*

December 21, 1976

February 14, 1978

GALLERY

DAN McMILLAN

TOWNSEND WOLFE

GEORGE ROSE SMITH

BOB HICKS

GALLERY

BILL SHELTON

BETTY BUMPERS

FRANK LAMBRIGHT

CHARLES ALLBRIGHT

JOE PURCELL

BILL CLINTON

Moral Commitment

April 10, 1975

Moral Commitment

We have been taught that to provide death-dealing weapons to certain countries is vital for peace. Mort Sahl was quoted as saying, "That's like making love to protect virginity."

We have provided the dictator of Iran billions of dollars in sophisticated weaponry. Iran would be a world power if it had the technical skills to operate them. We are committed to see that it gets that, too. We are by far the world's largest arms merchant. Candidate Carter back in '76 said he wanted the U.S. to be the world's granary—not the world's armory. No wonder the public is getting increasingly cynical about politics and government.

We arm both sides as if we were a good humor man, keeping everybody happy and contented.

We are still struggling with our consciences about the lessons we were supposed to learn in Southeast Asia. It makes one wonder—are we trying to buy peace, at any cost?

Just recently Carter agreed to provide nuclear devices to India, which exploded an atomic bomb in 1974, contrary to the agreement it made with Canada, which provided the nuclear research knowledge. Then we scold West Germany for selling the same stuff to Brazil. Soviet Russia is beset with horrendous problems, both domestic and global, and I'm sure she is amused by our jockeying to appease our so-called "allies."

What IS our role? Surely there must be another way of existing on this planet without arming every bailiwick to "defend" themselves.

Delmore Schwartz said, "Time is the school in which we learn. Time is the fire in which we burn."

Have Gun, Will Travel

February 20, 1975

"Our involvement will be limited to . . ."

February 11, 1975—The long travail in Vietnam was finally ended for the United States. Our efforts to help South Vietnam to maintain a formidable defense against possible invasion from the North didn't work. After we pulled out, North Vietnam invaded and President Ford appealed for aid in yet another effort to save South Vietnam.

April 15, 1975

Religious Note: Rev. Billy Graham finally sees the dark.

August 5, 1975

"Let's help the Americans celebrate their bicentennial. Let's charge $17.76 per barrel."

October 1, 1975

December 2, 1975

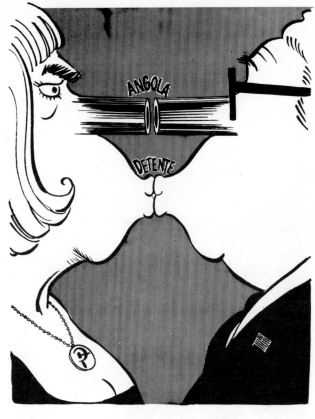

The KISSINGer Policy

December 30, 1975

July 13, 1976

July 8, 1976—Israel made a heroic rescue of hijacked airline passengers (mostly Jewish) from Entebbe airport in Dictator Idi Amin's Uganda. Amin had given the hijackers sanctuary. Adolph Hitler, Amin's hero, would have been proud of him.

"Sir! You forgot your trading stamps and charge card!"

August 10, 1976

70

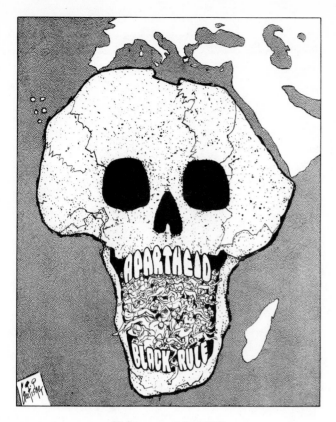

February 13, 1977

February 18, 1976

May 26, 1977—Congress wanted to build the B-1. Carter didn't want it, arguing that our present bombers could deliver the Cruise missile to its target with as much efficiency. As the overrun cost of the plane kept going up, ($100 million each) its previously touted performance expectations kept going down.

The B-1 Chorus

June 30, 1977

July 1, 1977

July 10, 1977

August 1, 1977

September 11, 1977

February 2, 1978—Middle East peace hopes dimmed when the Begin government continued to establish settlements in the territories Israel captured in the 1967 war.

"Speak up! I can't hear a word you're saying!"

February 3, 1978

February 23, 1978

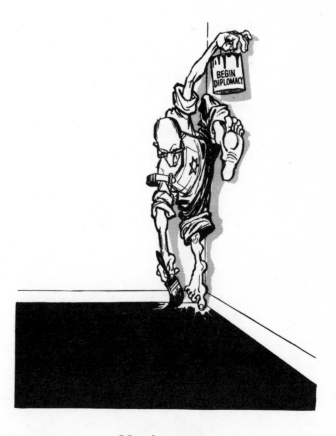

March 26, 1978

GALLERY

JIMMY CARTER

ROY MITCHELL

ERNIE DEANE

LEONA TROXELL

GALLERY

LARRY OBSITNIK

BOB DOUBLEDAY

DAVID PRYOR

JACK MERIWETHER

JASON ROUBY

BILL WALMSLEY

The U.S. Army Chorus of Engineers

April 2, 1978

God Would Have Done It
If He'd Had the Money

Here it is 1978 and we're still thinking in terms of building mammoth dams for flood control. Flood Control! That's the usual number one reason for damming a river. The "Keep Busy" boys still try to sell us the same old wad that constructing dams at enormous expense (both in dollars and environmental impact) is a high public priority need. But the public is ahead of the developers in the awareness that we have reached a saturation point with such projects. There have been other issues such as channelization, water and air standards and the use of pesticides and herbicides, just to name a few.

The battle to save the Cache River, North America's largest wintering habitat for the Mallard Duck, is still blazing. Lengthy studies have been made and counter proposals submitted to save the river's natural character and at the same time provide relief for flooded farmers upstream. Like good soldiers, however, the U.S. Army Engineers feels honor-bound to stick to the original ditching plan. Since the protracted Cache battle is so important, I am leading off this chapter with that series, then picking up with cartoons of other environmental and conservation concern.

Same Old Turkey

November 30, 1975

Consider the Work of God; For Who Can Make That Straight, Which He Hath Made Crooked? — Ecclesiastes 7:13

March 25, 1976—In court more than out, the Corps' plan finally got a green light.

"By dam — he'll know he's been in a fight!"

July 22, 1976—Presidential candidate Carter remarked that he was going to curb activities of the Corps.

February 22, 1977—After becoming president, Carter named 32 water projects he wanted killed or cut back. One of them was the Cache ditching project.

March 2, 1977—Meantime, the Corps had enough money to ditch 3.1 miles, and proceeded to do it.

March 9, 1977—Governor Pryor had just said no to the Bell Foley Dam plans, but, for unexplained reasons, would not take a stand on the Cache question.

There's one more party that hasn't been heard from . . .

March 31, 1977

Carter's Little River Pills
April 19, 1977

Mouse to Mouse Resuscitation

May 22, 1977—Congress got busy trying to force Carter to compromise. Congressman Bill Alexander did all he could to purge the Cache from Carter's list of projects to discontinue.

Dugout Dave

May 29, 1977

Solomon's Decision

June 28, 1977—Many Arkansans agonized over whether the Cache would be condemned in the compromise.

July 7, 1977—Meanwhile, the Corps kept ditching a small portion of the lower Cache.

An Innocent on Death Row

August 2, 1977—Congressional pressure forced Carter to reduce his list to seven. The Cache was not on the remaining list of projects to be discontinued.

August 10, 1977

April 27, 1978—Senator Bumpers dealt another blow to Alexander's and the Corps' plans. He vowed to block all funds for future ditching of the Cache.

March 17, 1978—Governor Pryor in a news conference surprised everyone by bringing up the Cache issue, but what he had to say was puzzling. He said that the money required to channelize the Cache should be spent on highways(!)

October 7, 1977—In ditching the river, the Corps realized that it had no place to deposit its silt, which was in violation of Section 404. This, plus the Arkansas Game and Fish Commission's refusal to give them right-of-way through the Dagmar Wildlife Area, started the ditchers to talking compromise.

September 1, 1974

"Arkansas has the same right to filthy air as the rest of the country."

March 4, 1975

"Go tell the governor we're ready for the dam."

March 30, 1975

It is finished. Let us pray . . . .

May 22, 1975

"Look at it this way, Chief—the Egyptians had to quit building pyramids, too!"

July 22, 1975—Governor Pryor announced that he was opposed to the Bell Foley Dam.

Pogo and his friends will soon depart.
— News item

June 29, 1975—The long-established comic strip Pogo had to leave the scene. Those who tried to keep it going after its creator, Walt Kelly, died just couldn't breathe life into the characters. I used artistic license to show why they may have left the swamps.

Dark shadows over another free-flowing stream.
May 12, 1976

'Isn't he cute? He's learned to catch them in mid-air."

July 13, 1975—For some time, the Arkansas Game and Fish Commission has shown a keen interest in mitigation land (substitute land offered by an agency to soften the impact of a project). So far as I know the Corps has not made good its mitigation offer for **any** project.

September 21, 1976

Dirty Old Men

February 15, 1976

Help on the way.

January 19, 1977—The Corps still wanted to build that dam on the Strawberry River, so the Assembly voted to revive it. Pryor stood fast.

January 28, 1977

March 18, 1977

March 27, 1977

"Al-ter-na-tive . . ."

April 10, 1977

April 24, 1977

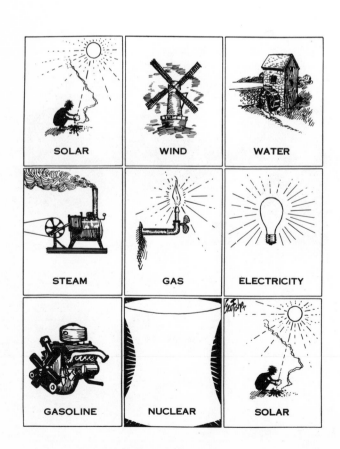

May 11, 1977

The second battle of Prairie Grove

June 3, 1977—The state's Parks and Tourism Department announced that it was going to build an amphitheater right on top of a battlefield site. Opposition cropped up everywhere and a retreat took place.

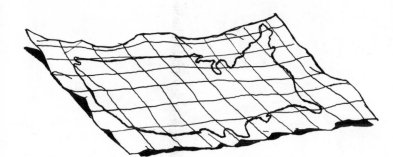

June 21, 1977

October 21, 1977—A government study revealed that some states were going to suffer water shortages. It recommended looking at the possibility of getting it from Arkansas, which has an abundant supply.

January 31, 1978—The Corps got the word. What Carter, Congress, EPA and the public had been telling it was to get born again.

"Don't get alarmed boys—this new way of growing cotton won't catch on."

November 15, 1977—Lily Peter, of Marvell, who is well known as a friend and protector of nature, is also a cotton farmer. She didn't like the poisonous pesticides spread all over, so she decided to grow her cotton without it. She got great results.

Conflict of Interest

January 18, 1978

Voice Crying in the Wilderness

January 27, 1978

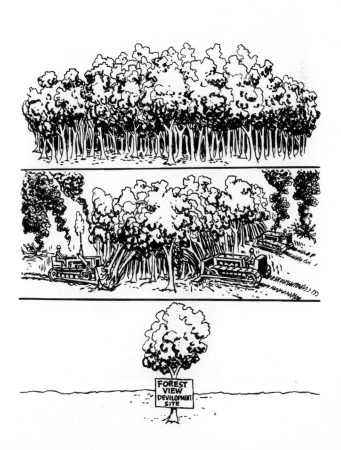

March 19, 1978

March 22, 1978

March 29, 1978

April 13, 1978

Viva La Snail Darter!

June 20, 1978

"What a coincidence. We were on our way to church, too."

June 1, 1975

June 8, 1978

June 27, 1978

Great Moments in History

June 30, 1978

GALLERY

WILBUR D. MILLS

PAUL GREENBERG

CAL LEDBETTER

BOB SCOTT

GALLERY

LOU HOLTZ

GUY "MUTT" JONES

BILL LEWIS

HENRY KISSINGER

April 5, 1977—Everyone was speculating as to who would enter the Senate contest but most forgot that John McClellan still held the seat and just might surprise all these young upstarts by running again.

Primary Pageant

The 1978 Arkansas Democratic primary was a dull affair for the most part until the last week or so of the Senate race.

Governor David Pryor, Congressmen Ray Thornton, Jim Guy Tucker and A. C. Grigson squared away in the May 30th primary. Pryor led the ticket but Tucker and Thornton were close behind. Tucker edged into second place but Pryor prevailed in the runoff.

The governor's race was hardly a contest. Bill Clinton eliminated four other opponents in the first primary with about 60% of the vote.

January 24, 1978

January 22, 1978—Arkansas, like many other states, found itself bulging with a big surplus in its coffers, but the governor didn't seem anxious to spend any of it.

February 16, 1978—There was no doubt as to whose candidacy would benefit most from the surplus.

March 9, 1978

April 19, 1978—Pryor had always enjoyed labor's support but this time Jim Guy got the endorsement. Tucker also was endorsed by the Arkansas Education Association.

May 12, 1978—31-year-old "Billy the Kid" Clinton seemed impregnable.

May 27, 1978

June 1, 1978

People who live in glass cookie jars...

June 4, 1978—Pryor led the Senate primary, Tucker was runner-up. Pryor wasted no time attacking his opponent as a captive of labor, charging that much of Jim Guy's campaign funds came from out-of-state labor organizations. Both candidates heaped praise on Ray Thornton, however.

June 7, 1978—Pryor declined to debate Tucker. No doubt he remembered his debate with Senator McClellan during the Senate race in 1972. Many observers believe that Big John saved the election for himself in that confrontation.

*ALIAS CHARLIE BROWN

June 16, 1978

GALLERY

BILL ALEXANDER

GEORGE WALLACE

RAY THORNTON

BILL SMITH

BOB FISHER

GALLERY

CHARLES BISHOP

ROBERT R. DOUGLAS

BEN ALLEN

FRANK HOLT

JOHN YANCEY

BETTY WOODS

September 30, 1977

Shoot-out at the Old Canal

The Panama Canal Treaties painfully squeaked through the U.S. Senate by the narrowist of margins.

It became an issue during the presidential campaign of 1976. After President Ford declared himself pro-treaties, Ronald Reagan siezed the opportunity and began beating him over the head with it. Ford prevailed by winning the Republican nomination. Democratic presidential candidate Carter soft-peddled the issue, but later, as president, led the successful fight for ratification.

"Yesterday we learned how to make a flaming shish kebab. Today . . . ."

May 28, 1976

August 16, 1977

Shoot-out at the old Canal

September 25, 1977—Hard-liner John Wayne surprised most people by taking a public stand FOR the treaties.

January 12, 1978

February 9, 1978

General McMath into the breach

February 26, 1978

Like a bridge over troubled waters

February 21, 1978

"Important duties in Washington preclude
my active campaign . . . OUCH!"

September 29, 1974

Hi, fellas! I'm back!

The tragic story of former Congressman Wilbur D. Mills is now history.

The bizarre reports that came out of his association with stripper Fanne Foxx and his drinking problem do not need to be retold in all its embarrassing detail.

After the Tidal Basin incident, Mills returned home to run for re-election against Republican Judy Petty. He revealed to the voters that he was an alcoholic but if the voters would return him to Washington, he would try to conquer his problem and get back into the swing of being chairman of the powerful Ways and Means Committee.

He won re-election, followed by one last fling with Fanne in Boston. The rest of his term was marked by obscurity. He was absent because for once he was seriously trying to whip his problem.

Much to his credit, he won that booze battle but retired from politics at the end of his term.

"Little Judy! My, how you've grown."

October 20, 1974

113

"Pinch me, Grace! Could that be the chairman of the powerful Ways and Means Committee?"

October 27, 1974

Taxation without representation

March 16, 1975

"Hi, fellas! I'm back!"

May 18, 1975

When it rains it pours

August 31, 1975

Mills' Seat

February 12, 1976

"I just love the ground I walk on."

September 12, 1975—Fanne Foxx continued to exploit her association with Wilbur Mills, doing every tinseled performance her agents could dream up.

GALLERY

JIM GUY TUCKER

ORVILLE HENRY

SID McMATH

RON MEYER

GENE WARREN

GALLERY

EDWIN C. KANE

CARRICK PATTERSON

DR. ROBERT LEFLAR

BETTY FULKERSON

"Don't do that!
People will think I intimidate you."

October 7, 1975

Don't Point That Thing at Me!

Publish an editorial cartoon favoring some sort of gun registration and you're a lead-pipe cinch to draw a barrage of fire, designed to make you feel ashamed for suggesting that people surrender all their firearms, leaving them defenseless against the criminals.

They say you're interfering with their constitutional right to bear arms. That's not exactly true. The writers of the original charter were referring to the states' right to maintain a militia, so say many subsequent rulings by the U.S. Supreme Court.

Another argument is that one day they might have to give up their hunting weapons. What kind of game do you hunt with a Saturday Night Special?

Guns don't kill legislation—
CONGRESSMEN kill gun legislation.

February 16, 1977

*When you outlaw
student guns
only outlaw students
will have guns*

November 27, 1974—A student was wounded by a gunshot from another student in a Little Rock secondary school. The incident exposed a problem that the public didn't know about: a number of students carried guns to school.

There were immediate demands for a crackdown, but some students thought they had a right to carry a weapon and that the law did not permit school officials to search them.

"Hey! Don't point that thing at ME!"

October 29, 1975

For about 25 bucks you, too, can own your own business.

July 22, 1977

Don't complain—
he has a legal right to own it.

November 30, 1976—In November, 1976, my wife and I drove to a Little Rock motel to visit friends just after dark. After we got out of our car, two young men walked up to us and blocked our path. One, brandishing a small shiny pistol, ordered me to drop my wallet, which I did. The other grabbed my wife's purse as both disappeared into the darkness.

The above cartoon was drawn a few days later. It portrays the punk who held the gun on me.

GALLERY

JIM POWELL

MARGARET CARNER

ED DUNAWAY

RICHARD M. NIXON

GALLERY

JON KENNEDY

WILLIAM KIRBY

PAUL VAN DALSEM

JOHN THOMPSON

TOM GLAZE

DEPENDENCE ON
FOREIGN FUEL

May 13, 1977

Yankee Dollar

Perhaps it is unnecessary for me to explain our world economic situation. That's ridiculous. I don't think I understand it myself.

I do understand, however, that we are at the mercy of a few Middle-East sheikdoms because we're hooked on oil.

When I was growing up I was taught that the U.S. was the world's greatest oil producer. But we didn't use as much oil back then. Now we are told that we must import oil to survive. Meanwhile, prices soar, wages increase, profits rise—and the cow is jumping over the moon.

Okay, you say, let's come to our senses.

What we need is an overall energy policy to determine what we have, how we are going to use it and, in general, where we are going.

Over a year ago, President Carter proposed such a plan, but at this writing Congress still seems reluctant to fight its way through the lobby jungle to grapple with **anybody's** plan.

Historically, Congress has moved like an arthritic turtle on such matters. Let us hope it will make some sort of response before we are engulfed by a national crisis.

The Upper House

June 14, 1977

Umbilical Cord

September 19, 1976—The U.S. Senate Ethics Committee, with some of its most powerful members steeped in the Gulf Oil political contribution question, purged itself of any wrongdoing in this potentially damaging scandal.

October 14, 1977

"I'm not sure I want ANY of you tramping on my bridge," said the troll.

November 21, 1976

December 18, 1977

Removal of the Troll

January 3, 1978

February 8, 1978

December 16, 1977

130

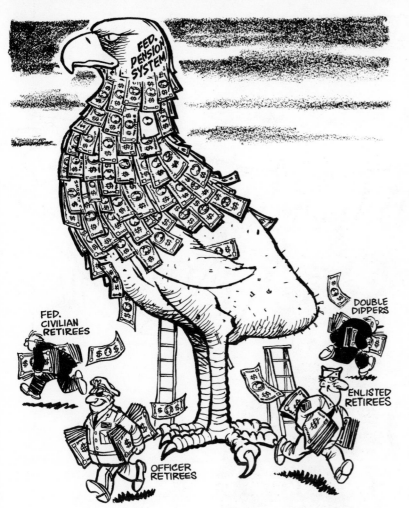

March 22, 1978

Middle Man

April 6, 1978

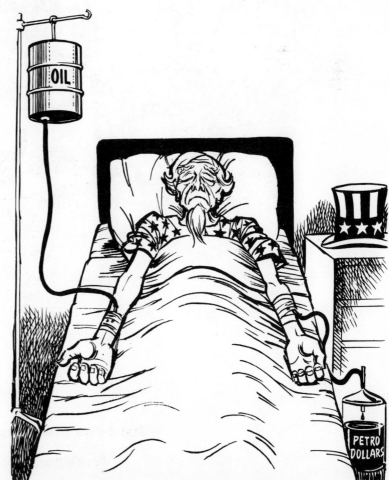

"Have you tried the pill?"

January 5, 1975

Thank God fo' Arkansas!

Arkansas seems to have more trouble financing schools than other states.

One of the major reasons is that we're not as rich as most others. Another is that we rank 50th in the nation in state and local taxes paid per capita. Some statistics show that we now rank 50th (below Mississippi) in average teacher salaries. Our schools, too, are victims of our badly structured tax system. The assessment of property tax in Arkansas is a jungle of discrimination.

As if our state colleges and universities weren't having enough trouble squeezing funds from our legislature, two-year community colleges started springing up like toad-stools.

Then the 1975 General Assembly, in its collective wisdom, put through a bill authorizing scholarship grants to private colleges. Currently, the U.S. Congress has a plan in the works that would give tuition tax credit to primary and secondary schools including church and private schools. Let us pray.

What would all this do to our public schools, to say nothing of our Constitution?

"Mind turning your light off just for a second?"

December 22, 1974

"What the founding fathers have rent asunder, let us now join together."

March 5, 1975

June 5, 1975

"Sic 'im, Fido!"

September 28, 1976

Frank of the Ozarks

December 31, 1975

December 10, 1976

Satellite

May 20, 1977

February 7, 1978

April 12, 1978

May 18, 1978

February 15, 1978

GALLERY

ROBERT S. McCORD

WILLIE OATES

WALTER E. HUSSMAN, JR.

ROGER MEARS

GERALD FORD

GALLERY

MARLIN HAWKINS

B. FINLEY VINSON

BOBBIE FORRESTER

MAX HOWELL

RALPH PATRICK

JIM RANCHINO

The Guilty

The Innocent

August 17, 1975

The Guilty and the Innocent

On the following pages are a few cartoons dealing with law, courts and law enforcement.

The Rockefeller tenure in Arkansas ushered in our Freedom of Information law. Since then state boards, commissions and agencies have been slow in getting used to opening the doors any time they meet as a body. It's a good law but it is constantly in jeopardy of being chopped up by law-makers.

On the national scene, the post-Watergate period saw big corporations hauled into court and fined for illegal political contributions. But what about those who received the money? They're guilty, too, but they're rarely convicted.

The U. S. Supreme Court, with four Nixon appointees, many times finds at least one recruit from the remaining five to hand down some very disappointing rulings, as if they were orchestrated by the old master of dirty tricks himself.

"Be careful to cut out only the part that involves us."

October 6, 1974

"Now let's go over it one more time."

May 25, 1975—The University of Arkansas Board of Trustees, of all people, had to be repeatedly warned by the Arkansas Supreme Court to quit meeting in private.

November 26, 1975—For years, the courts have, in many cases, issued orders restraining the press from writing stories about trials until the verdict is given. Also, many reporters have been jailed for not naming the source of their stories to grand juries.

*"The mean old press just won't leave us
alone . . . It's more than us honest,
dedicated public servants can bear."*

December 7, 1975

"Give Me Your Poor, Your Blacks, Your Social Pariahs..."

January 11, 1976—No matter what you think of the death penalty, it is not meted out fairly by our society. If you are rich, white, pleasant-looking — and, yes, female — the chances of your getting executed are less. We should end capital punishment until this discrimination is erased.

June 22, 1977—Circuit Judge Means of Malvern pulled the rug from under the jury and prosecutor when he fined and suspended three men who were caught with several hundred pounds of marijuana. It set off a blast of indignation heard all over Arkansas.

Later, however, the case was channeled into Federal Court, where a much sterner conviction was meted out.

April 28, 1977

September 4, 1977—The furor over the Judge Means case was so intense that the legislature debated impeachment. The law-makers don't like to make such decisions, so they referred the matter to the legislative Joint Interim Committee on Legislative Affairs to study the Means case and make a report.

The committee recommended censuring him, which amounted to almost nothing, so the Judge went back to the bench.

November 4, 1977—In 1976, Candidate Jimmy Carter promised that "Big Shot Crooks" would not get off with token sentences.

In 1977, Richard Helms, Director of the CIA during the Nixon administration, was hauled into court on a raft of charges, but the Justice Department allowed him to plea bargain down to one, so Mr. Helms got off with a light fine and a suspended sentence.

"You're right! That thing is blinding! Heaven knows how you're able to get your work done."

January 25, 1976

June 11, 1978

GALLERY

J. WILLIAM FULBRIGHT

RONALD REAGAN

TOM SPARKS

BETTY FOWLER

DALE BUMPERS

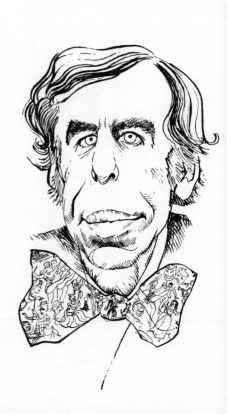

PHILIP G. BACK

GALLERY

WAYNE CRANFORD

BOB CAREY

LEROY DONALD

WINTHROP PAUL ROCKEFELLER

NOLAND BLASS

September 2, 1977

Farkleberry Favorites

Many cartoons were published within the last four years that don't fit into any of the previous categories. I would be remiss if I left out any of what, I think, are readers' favorites.

July 20, 1977

"... and do you solemnly promise to do absolutely nothing?"

January 1, 1975—When Dale Bumpers was elected to the U.S. Senate, he resigned as governor a week early to somehow gain seniority in Congress. He was obviously uneasy that Lt. Gov. Bob Riley, in his mini-tenure, might do something he would not approve of.

May 11, 1975—We've had a rough time with constitutional reforms in Arkansas. Every time it looks like it might get off the ground, something shoots it down. This time it was the courts. They didn't approve of the architects' plan.

Outrigger

June 22, 1975

The Shoe Must Go On

August 24, 1975

Led Neck

May 20, 1975—When South Vietnam was overrun by the North, refugees fled to the United States and other countries. Former President Ky was among them. After arriving in the U.S., he was quoted as saying he might become an Arkansas farmer.

September 21, 1975—The big folk center was heralded as a step forward in preserving Arkansas's precious folk culture. The federal government spent more than a million dollars building it, but soon after the doors were open, the musicians and others started bolting. What's a music hall without musicians?

December 14, 1975

"Ever think about running for political office?"

April 18, 1976—The Arkansas GOP was desperate to get people to run for office. It even asked Orval Faubus to run for governor as a Republican.

"For Two Cents I'd Quit Watching This Trash!"

February 17, 1976

Shotgun . . . wedding?

April 20, 1976

"You take a sharp left at Walnut Corner."

May 14, 1977—Chase Manhattan Bank ran an ad proclaiming that there was no imminent money shortage because of government restrictions as they affected private enterprise. Its officials said they would debate anyone anywhere who disagreed. Bob Sitarzewski of Helena challenged them and Chase had to come through. A team traveled all the way from New York to Helena to debate.

"I see — an eleventh-hour endorsement by you and there won't be any nasty, last-minute editorials or cartoons."

June 8, 1976—Pulaski County Judge Mackey was retiring and Little Rock Mayor Wimberly was locked in a runoff with Roger Mears. In the waning hours, Mackey surprised everyone by announcing his choice. Wimberly lost.

June 16, 1976

Here's to the Highway Commission
That dabbles in cement and sod
Where the Governor speaks only to the Commission
And the Commission speaks only to God.

July 14, 1977

September 2, 1976

August 30, 1977—A television station gave its news anchor-man the axe because ratings were not what it would like them to be. Needless to say, other TV newsmen became nervous at the prospects of what could easily happen to them.

August 31, 1977

All those in favor of a 50¢ zoo fee, hold up your hand.

November 9, 1977

September 1, 1977—John Preston had been a popular director of Little Rock's Museum of Science and History for a long time. He worked hard at providing demonstrations and lectures on natural history in schools and other institutions all over the city. The Board asked him to resign, which set off a public furor. He was accused of not following the Board's guidelines on how the Museum should be run. There was an obvious conflict of policy and personality. Preston finally lost his job, but the controversy proved how many admirers he had.

September 16, 1977—A severe storm caused electricity to go out in many parts of Little Rock, including the AP&L's office headquarters.

Oh! Fort Smith!

March 21, 1978—The crude skin show, "Oh! Calcutta!" made its swing through Arkansas, playing first in Little Rock, then in Fort Smith. The show was too far-out for Fort Smith's sensibilities, so the cast was hauled in and fined.

July 5, 1978

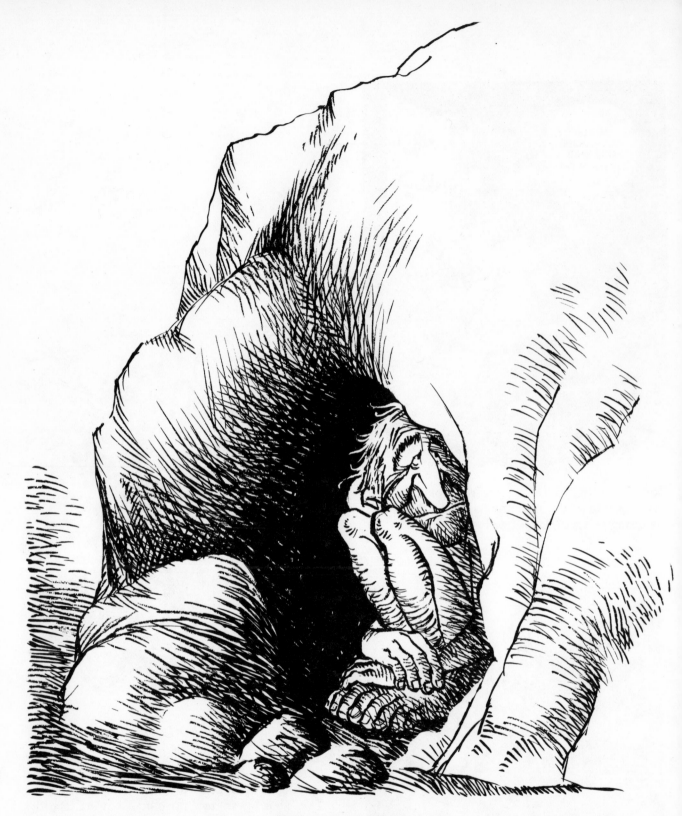

Rabbit Hole No. 2

March 7, 1978—Poor Orval has had his troubles lately. His wife was given several tickets and warnings by local police for speeding. She charged that the police harrassed her and roughed her up a bit, and she decided to air it out in court.

At the trial, she was fined and lectured by the judge. Afterward, a local newspaper photographer tried to get a shot of the Faubuses, and Orval allegedly grabbed the camera and threw it down some steps, breaking it.

Some other unpleasant things happened, but the photographer, a female relative of Orval's ex-wife, filed charges, which were later dropped after the Faubuses agreed to pay for damages.

Faubus then put his home and property up for sale for $1,100,000, and announced that he would leave the state as soon as he sold his house.

Those who remember Faubus as governor recall his pet phrase: "I always have a second rabbit hole to run to in case the first one is blocked."